Level B

Writing
— for —
Proficiency

A Test Preparation Program

GLOBE FEARON
EDUCATIONAL PUBLISHER
PARAMUS, NEW JERSEY

Paramount

Paramount Publishing

Executive Editor: Barbara Levadi
Editorial Developer: Curriculum Concepts, Inc.
Production Director: Penny Gibson
Manufacturing Supervisor: Della Smith
Senior Production Editor: Linda Greenberg
Production Editor: Alan Dalgleish
Marketing Manager: Sandra Hutchison
Electronic Interior Design: Curriculum Concepts, Inc.
Art Director: Nancy Sharkey
Cover Design: BB&K Design Inc.

Printed in the United States of America
3 4 5 6 7 8 9 10   99 98 97 96

ISBN: 0-835-90892-5

GLOBE FEARON
EDUCATIONAL PUBLISHER
PARAMUS, NEW JERSEY

Paramount Publishing

Introduction

Unit 1: Writing For the Essay Test

Chapter 1: The Three Elements of Good Writing

Chapter 2: Four Types of Essays

Unit 2: Improving Your Score

Chapter 1: Planning Your Essay

Chapter 2: Strategies for Clear and Interesting Writing

Chapter 3: Mechanics and Usage

Chapter 4: Revising and Proofreading

Unit 3: Preparing to Take the Writing Test

SUCCEEDING ON THE WRITING TEST

Soon you'll be taking your state's writing test. So will many other students in the state. There are three big questions that students wonder about as they prepare for the test. This book is going to answer those questions.

THREE BIG QUESTIONS

1. What's Going to Be on the Test?

- You're going to be asked to write an essay. Most tests will give a written assignment called a **prompt**. Here's an example of a prompt you might be asked to respond to:

> *Your school is canceling a word-processing course. It will buy new uniforms for the sports teams instead. Do you agree or disagree with this plan?*

- The test may also include questions and will give you a choice of answers. This is a **multiple-choice test**. Here's an example of a multiple-choice question:

Direction: Read the sentence. One of the underlined parts is incorrect. Choose the letter that shows where the mistake is.

A	B	C	D

The <u>books</u> that Willy is <u>reading</u> <u>are</u> <u>mine's</u>.

Ⓐ A   Ⓒ C
Ⓑ B   Ⓓ D

This book will give you many opportunities to write essays. You'll learn what a good essay is all about. And you'll get a chance to practice some strategies that will help you write a successful essay based on your own good ideas. You'll also learn about multiple-choice tests and strategies to help you do well on them.

2. How Am I Going to Be Graded?

A reader will score your writing test. That reader is specially trained to evaluate your writing. Here are some points the reader will look for in your essay.

- Does the essay answer the prompt clearly and completely?
- Is the writing clear and to the point?
- Is the essay well organized?
- Does the essay give reasons that support its ideas?
- Does the essay contain good grammar, spelling, and punctuation?

This book will help you learn what you need to know to answer "Yes!" to all of these questions. You'll learn how to plan and write a well-organized essay. You'll also learn how to tell if you have written one.

3. What Do I Have to Do to Get a Good Grade?

The answer to this question is BE PREPARED! These ideas will help you.

- Practice writing as much and as often as you can. The more you write, the better you'll become at writing.
- Learn how to recognize and correct your mistakes.
- Have confidence in yourself. You have good ideas. You can learn how to write about those ideas.
- Learn how much time you can give to each part of the test.

You will see this clock on some pages of this book. It is there to remind you that most writing tests will be timed. The time on the clock is to give you an idea of how much time you would have if you were taking the test.

Now it's time for you to begin making sure that you succeed on your writing test. Remember, you can do it!

U N I T 1

WRITING FOR THE ESSAY TEST

What Is an Essay?

An **essay** is a short piece of writing in which you say what you think about a topic.

The person who grades the test will expect to see that your essay contains these four elements:

1. The **central idea**: the essay's main idea. Your whole essay concerns this idea.

2. The **introduction**: the opening paragraph. You should state the essay's central idea in this paragraph.

3. The **body**: two or more paragraphs that follow the introduction. Each of these paragraphs should give details about the central idea.

4. The **closing**: the last paragraph. In the closing, you should repeat the central idea in slightly different words.

This picture can help you remember how an essay is organized.

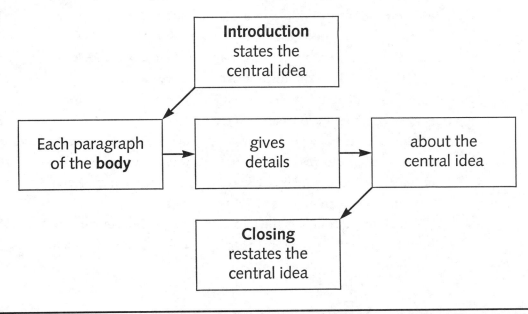

CHAPTER 1 THE THREE ELEMENTS OF GOOD WRITING

Knowing and using these three keys to good writing will help you get a better grade on your writing test.

- **Focus** Everything in your essay should be about your central idea.
- **Support** Give details that back up your central idea.
- **Organization** Begin with the central idea. Give details. Then repeat the central idea in your closing paragraph.

LESSON 1

A Good Essay

Read this prompt. Then read the essay carefully. Think about how the writer uses the three elements of good writing—focus, support, and organization—to write a good essay.

Check It Out

> *Your school is canceling a word-processing course. It will buy new uniforms for the sports teams instead. Do you agree or disagree with this plan?*

I think the school is making a mistake. It should not cancel	1
the word-processing course. Even though I agree that our teams	2
need new uniforms, I think we need the course more.	3
Uniforms look good on the players, but only the players use	4
them. Learning word processing may not make anyone look	5
good, but it's a skill that lots of us can use. We can use word	6
processing for compositions for school. We can also use it for	7
personal writing like journals and letters.	8
Many of us may need to know word processing to get jobs	9
later on. New uniforms won't help us get jobs. We need to look	10
ahead. Word processing is one way to begin using a computer.	11
Computer skills can help us to get better jobs.	12
Canceling the course is the wrong way to go. The course will	13
do the most good for the most people. It will help us now and in	14
the future.	15

Work It Out

Look back at the essay. Here are some examples of how the writer uses focus, support, and organization.

Focus

- In lines 1-2, the writer answers the prompt. The writer's opinion is that the school is making a mistake by canceling the word-processing course. The writer has given the central idea of the essay.
- Every sentence in the essay is about the central idea.

Support

- Details that support the central idea can be reasons, facts, and examples. In the first paragraph, the writer gives one reason for not canceling the course. The writer says that students need the course more than they need new uniforms.
- In lines 5-8, the writer gives the example that students can use word processing for schoolwork and for personal writing.
- In lines 9-12, the writer states the fact that word processing is one way to begin learning to use a computer. The writer also points out that computer skills are important to getting good jobs.
- In lines 13-15, the writer gives almost a tiny version of the whole essay. The writer restates the central idea and the supporting ideas.

Organization

- In lines 1-3, the writer presents the central idea of the essay.
- In lines 4-12, the writer presents details that support the central idea of the essay.
- In lines 13-15, the writer repeats the central idea and restates the supporting details.

Look It Over

Think about focus, support, and organization. Which of these three keys to good writing do you find hardest? Explain why.

_____

_____

_____

_____

_____

_____

Focus Your Writing

After deciding on your central idea, you must stay with it. All the information you put in the essay should be about the central idea. Ask yourself whether each sentence concerns the central idea. Your answer to this question will help you **focus** your writing. If you're uncertain, maybe that sentence doesn't belong.

Check It Out

Read the following prompt and essay. Look for sentences that don't fit with the writer's central idea. Then answer the questions.

> *Some people believe that television can be a bad influence on young children. Do you agree or disagree? Why?*

Television is more of a good influence on children than a bad	1
influence. I guess it's true that some kids watch more TV than	2
they should. But still, they're better off than they would be if	3
they didn't have anything to watch.	4
Students can learn a lot from television. When I was in sev-	5
enth grade, I watched a program about Arctic seals. The next day	6
I gave an oral report in class about seals and got an "A." Two of	7
my classmates also got good grades on their reports. One report	8
was about how farmers grow wheat The other was about flags.	9
Television also keeps kids from doing things they shouldn't be	10
doing. My best friend has a TV in his living room and a small	11
one in his kitchen. If some kids weren't watching television, they	12
might get into trouble by roaming the streets or joining a gang.	13
Watching TV has a good effect on children	14

Work It Out

1. Read the first sentence. Then put the writer's central idea into your own words.

   _____

   _____

2. In line 5 the writer says that students learn from television Is this thought related to the central idea? Why or why not?

   _____

   _____

3. In lines 7-8 the writer says that other people also got good grades. Is this thought related to the central idea? Why or why not?

_____

_____

_____

4. What other sentences in that paragraph are not focused on the central idea?

_____

_____

_____

5. In lines 10-13, what sentence **does not** tell more about the central idea?

_____

_____

_____

6. What else could you add to the closing paragraph to make the essay more persuasive?

_____

_____

_____

Look It Over

Look back at your answers to questions 1-5. Then write a tip that will help you keep your focus as you plan and write an essay.

_____

_____

_____

_____

_____

_____

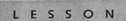# Support Your Ideas

A good essay writer supports the central idea with details. Details help make your central idea clear and convincing. Three types of details you can use are:

- **facts:** details that can be proven
- **examples:** details that give more information
- **reasons:** details that tell how or why

Check It Out

Read the following prompt and essay. Think about how well each sentence supports the central idea. Then answer the questions.

> *Do you believe that parents should set curfews for their teenage children? Why or why not?*

Parents should not set a curfew for teenagers on weekend	1
nights. Teenagers are old enough to know when to come home	2
and go to bed.	3
In the first place, people who are sixteen or seventeen years	4
old are almost adults. They should be treated that way. My	5
friend's mother still treats her like she's eleven, even though my	6
friend is a really responsible person.	7
If there's no school the next day, there's really no need to be	8
in bed by a special time.	9
Most parents worry more than they should. They should learn	10
to relax a little bit. Teenagers are not always out in dangerous	11
situations.	12
A curfew is like having a bedtime. I think teenagers are way	13
past that stage. I think parents should let their teenagers decide	14
when to come home and go to bed on weekends.	15

Work It Out

1. Read lines 1-3. Then restate the writer's central idea in your own words.

_____

_____

_____

_____

2. Choose one thought from the essay that supports the writer's central idea. Write it below in your own words.

_____

_____

_____

3. According to lines 6-7, the writer's friend is responsible. Does the writer support this thought? How could the writer support it?

_____

_____

_____

_____

4. How could you support the thought in lines 8-9?

_____

_____

_____

_____

5. Which sentence in lines 10-12 supports the idea that parents worry more than they should? What other details might the writer add to this paragraph?

_____

_____

_____

_____

Look It Over

When you write an essay of your own, how will you judge if you have included enough supporting details?

_____

_____

_____

_____

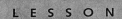

LESSON 4 Organize Your Writing

When you write an essay, it is important to put your ideas and thoughts in order. Organizing your essay in this way helps the reader understand what you are saying.

You might be asked to describe an important event in your life. You can organize your ideas by writing about the things that happened in the order in which they happened. You can organize the details you give about each part of the event. Give the most important detail first and the least important detail last. Doing these things will help make your ideas easy to follow.

Check It Out

Read the following prompt and essay. Think about whether the paragraphs are well organized. Then answer the questions.

> *Describe an action that is completed in a number of steps. Explain the process and why it is important to know about it.*

It takes a number of steps to deliver a letter. That is why	1
it is important to address an envelope the right way.	2
Sometimes you have to make sure a letter gets to an	3
apartment in a large building. Write the apartment number	4
on the envelope. This will make sure the letter goes in the right	5
mailbox. Put the street address on the envelope to get the letter	6
to the right building.	7
The U. S. Postal Service uses every part of an address to	8
deliver a letter to the right place. A post office worker looks	9
at the ZIP code. When the letter gets to the right part of the	10
country, another post office sends it to the correct local post	11
office. The digits tell what part of the country the letter	12
should go to.	13
Think about all this the next time you address	14
an envelope. The people at the post office can't guess where	15
you want your letter to go. You have to address the envelope	16
so they know.	17
At the local post office, someone checks the street address.	18
That person puts the letter into a slot for that street. Then the	19
mail carrier picks up all the letters for that street.	20

Work It Out

1. What is the central idea of this essay?

   _____

   _____

2. The essay explains the three steps it takes to deliver a letter. In what order does the writer give these steps?

   _____

   _____

   _____

3. Now think about how these steps actually happen. List them in the order in which they happen.

   _____

   _____

   _____

4. If this were your essay, how would you organize the paragraphs to help the reader?

   _____

   _____

   _____

5. Look carefully at lines 8-13. Which sentence would you move to make the paragraph easier to understand?

   _____

   _____

Look It Over

Write yourself a tip for organizing an essay that describes a number of steps.

_____

_____

_____

_____

Put Your Learning Into Practice

In a good essay, the writer states the central idea in the introduction. Each paragraph in the body includes a thought about the central idea. In the closing the writer restates the central idea.

Check It Out

Read this prompt and essay. Then answer the questions that follow.

> *At what age can a person in your state get a driver's license? In your opinion, is this age limit fair? Why or why not?*

In my state a person can't get a driver's license until age	1
eighteen. I think this is unfair.	2
I don't think everyone should have to wait until age eighteen	3
to get a license. People can vote when they're eighteen, and boys	4
can get drafted into the army.	5
People don't grow up at the same speed. Some people at age	6
sixteen are even more responsible than people who are eighteen.	7
If you are responsible and tall enough to drive safely, you	8
should be able to get a license. I'm sixteen, and I'm already as	9
tall as my dad.	10
Cars also are a lot safer now than they were a long time ago.	11
People are different. They shouldn't all be judged as if they	12
are the same. Also, some teenagers need to drive more than	13
other teenagers. If I could get a license, I could get to school	14
in about fifteen minutes. If I could choose a car, I would get	15
a red convertible.	16
People should be able to get licenses because they need to	17
drive and because they will be careful. It's not fair to punish	18
people because of when they were born.	19

Work It Out

1. What is the central idea of the essay?

_____

_____

_____

_____

2. What thoughts about the central idea does the writer include? Write the details that support each thought

_____

_____

_____

_____

_____

3. In lines 3-10, what sentences are **not** focused on the central idea?

_____

_____

_____

4. What sentences should be followed with more supporting details?

_____

_____

_____

5. The writer repeats some ideas in more than one place. Tell why reorganizing these sentences would improve the essay.

_____

_____

_____

Look It Over

Write yourself a tip to help you remember how to improve the focus, organization, and support of an essay.

_____

_____

_____

_____

_____

_____

CHAPTER 2 · FOUR TYPES OF ESSAYS

This chapter teaches you to write four types of essays that are on most writing tests. The four essay types are **persuasive**, **descriptive**, **expository**, and **narrative**.

LESSON 1 · What Are the Different Types of Essays?

PERSUASIVE ESSAY

In a **persuasive essay**, you give an opinion about something and try to convince the reader to share it.

The prompt

The prompt for a persuasive essay might state an idea that people might support or not support. It might ask you to give your opinion about the idea and to back it up with reasons, facts, and examples.

Words to look for in the prompt

- agree
- disagree
- issue
- argue
- opinion
- persuade

> *Students should go to school all year long. Instead of closing for two months in the summer, schools would close four times a year for two weeks at a time. Do you agree or disagree?*

Your goal

To give an opinion and make the reader agree with it.

The plan

- Read the prompt. Underline important words or ideas.
- Decide what you think about the topic. What's your opinion?
- Think of two or three **reasons** to support your opinion.
- Use **examples** and **facts** to support your opinion.

Another example

Editorials in newspapers are persuasive essays.

DESCRIPTIVE ESSAY

In a **descriptive essay**, you describe a person, place, or thing.

The prompt

The prompt in a writing test may ask you to describe something or someone. It may also ask you to support your description with details.

Words to look for in the prompt

- describe
- description
- details
- important

> *Write a paragraph describing something funny about an adult you know.*

Your goal

- To give the reader a clear idea of what you're describing.
- To help the reader experience what you're describing.

The plan

- Read the prompt and decide what you're going to **describe.**
- List **words and phrases** that describe your subject.
- Use your five **senses** to get more ideas for your description. Think of words and phrases that tell how the person, place, or object looks, sounds, feels, smells, or tastes.
- Put your list of details in an **order** that will make them easy for the reader to understand.

Another example

Travel articles in newspapers and magazines contain descriptive writing.

Think It Over

What will be hardest for you about writing a descriptive essay? Write your thoughts on the lines below.

_____

_____

_____

_____

_____

EXPOSITORY ESSAY

In an **expository essay**, you explain something or give information about a topic.

The prompt

The prompt may ask you to explain what a certain word means to you. Or it might ask you to explain how to do something. Or it might ask you to explain how two things are alike or different.

Words to look for in the prompt

- define
- discuss
- alike, different
- explain
- process
- problem

> *Think of a useful invention. Write an essay explaining why you think the invention is useful.*

Your goal

To explain or give information about something to a reader.

The plan

- Read the prompt and decide what you will explain. If possible, choose something that you know something about.
- List all the things you know about your topic.
- Organize your details so that the reader will understand your ideas. Use words such as *first*, *next*, *then*, and *finally* to help your reader follow your thoughts.

Another example

You can find examples of expository writing in an encyclopedia. An encyclopedia is made up of essays that give information about topics.

Think It Over

What do you think will be the most challenging part of writing an expository essay? Write your thoughts on the lines below.

_____

_____

_____

_____

NARRATIVE ESSAY

In a **narrative essay**, you tell a story. The story can be real or made up.

The prompt

The prompt might ask you to tell something that really happened to you. Or it might ask you to make up a story.

Words to look for in the prompt

- experience
- remember
- tell
- event
- episode
- relate
- story
- real life

> *Think of an event when someone surprised you by doing something unexpected. Relate what happened during this experience.*

Your goal

To tell a story, either one from real life or one you make up.

The plan

- Read the prompt and decide what story you want to tell.
- List the actions or events that happen in your story. Where and when did these events take place?
- What characters are there in your story? What did people do or say? What did you think about as events happened?
- Organize these details. Tell what happened first, next, and last.
- Think about why this story has meaning for you. Did you learn something or change in some way during the story? Do you want to share with the reader a lesson you learned?

Another example

Biographies contain examples of narrative writing. A biography tells many episodes from a person's life.

Think It Over

How is a movie like a narrative essay?

_____

_____

_____

_____

_____

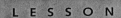

How to Write a Persuasive Essay

Here's a prompt for a persuasive essay that you might find on a writing test.

> *Some people think that students should go to school all year long. Instead of closing for two months during the summer, schools would close four times a year for two weeks at a time. What is your opinion?*

In a persuasive essay, you give your opinion and support it with reasons and examples. Look at this **opinion chart**.

Opinion: I believe that students should go to school all year long and have several short vacations instead of one long vacation.
Reason 1: American students need to catch up with students in other countries. **Example:** Japanese students don't have a long summer vacation, and they're ahead of American students.
Reason 2: Over the summer, we forget what we've learned. **Example:** The first month of school is usually a review of what we've forgotten during the summer.

Here's part of a persuasive essay. Can you find in the essay any reasons and examples from the chart above?

> I believe that we should have school all year, with short breaks instead of one long summer vacation.
>
> We need more school days to catch up with students in other countries. The school year is longer in Japan, France, and Russia than it is here. Students in these countries are ahead of us, especially in science and math.

What fact did the writer add to the essay that isn't in the chart?

_____

_____

_____

Plan a Persuasive Essay

Now you try planning a persuasive essay. Read the prompt below.

> *Think of an activity that people your age aren't usually allowed to do. Write an essay that gives reasons why people your age should be allowed to do this activity.*

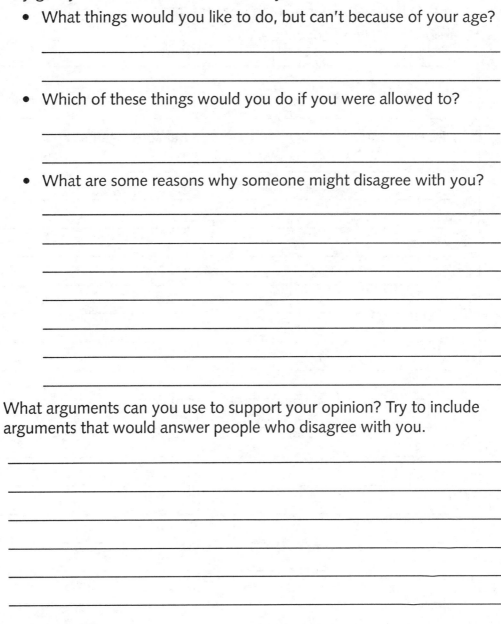

Start Out

Think about your own interests and experiences. The questions below may give you some ideas. Add ideas of your own.

- What things would you like to do, but can't because of your age?

  _____

  _____

- Which of these things would you do if you were allowed to?

  _____

- What are some reasons why someone might disagree with you?

  _____

  _____

  _____

  _____

  _____

What arguments can you use to support your opinion? Try to include arguments that would answer people who disagree with you.

_____

_____

_____

_____

_____

_____

Put It Together

Now that you've picked a topic and have come up with some ideas, you're ready to make your own chart. Here are some ideas to help you plan your essay.

- Think of two or three reasons that support your opinion. Provide examples or facts to back up your reasons. Also write some reasons why people might not agree with you. You can add other reasons if you think they are important.

- Put your reasons in order of their importance. Put the most important reason first and the least important reason last.

Fill in the chart with your opinion, reasons, facts, and examples.

Your opinion will be your central idea.

Your opinion: _____	
Reasons for:	**Reasons against:**
1._____	1._____
2._____	2._____
3._____	3._____

Write Your Essay

Use the chart to write your persuasive essay.

Here are some ideas to think about.

- Remember to give your central idea in the first paragraph.
- Start a new paragraph for each reason that supports your opinion.
- In each paragraph give examples or facts to support your opinion.
- You can mention and argue against ideas that are different from your own.
- In the closing paragraph, give the central idea again in a way that ties your reasons together. One way to do this is to say, "For all these reasons, I feel that. . . ."

Use a separate sheet of paper for your essay.

Look It Over

When you've finished writing, read your essay carefully. Then use this checklist to evaluate what you have written. Don't worry about spelling or grammar for now.

Circle a number on the scoring scale after each question. (**5** is the highest you can score; **1** is the lowest.)

Is the central idea clearly stated in the opening paragraph?

1   2   3   4   5

Does each paragraph give a new reason that supports the central idea?

1   2   3   4   5

Is each reason supported by an example or a fact?

1   2   3   4   5

Are your reasons listed in their order of importance?

1   2   3   4   5

Does the closing paragraph restate the central idea?

1   2   3   4   5

Think It Over

If you had to write this essay again, how would you change it? Write your ideas on the lines below.

_____

_____

_____

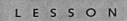

LESSON **3** **How to Write a Descriptive Essay**

Here's a prompt for a descriptive essay that might appear on a writing test.

> *Write a paragraph describing something funny about an adult you know.*

One writer decided to describe his father making soup. The writer made a **detail web** to help him come up with ideas for his description.

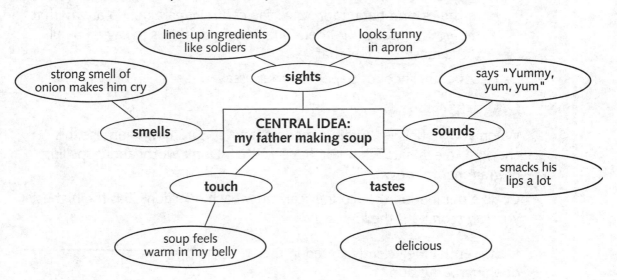

Compare the detail web with this paragraph from a descriptive essay.

    It's so funny to watch my father make soup. First he puts on an apron that's much too small for him. Then he lines up everything he needs in a row like little soldiers. When he chops the onions, the smell makes him look like he's crying. When he's almost finished with the soup, he tastes it, smacks his lips loudly, and says in a silly voice, "Yummy, yum, yum." I always say, "Dad, you're so weird." But then I laugh. He's usually not wrong. His soup is good, especially on those cold days when a hot bowl of soup makes you feel warm inside.

Which details from the web does the writer use in this paragraph?

_____

_____

_____

Plan a Descriptive Essay

Now you plan a descriptive essay. Use the prompt below.

> *Choose a favorite object of yours and write a description of this item. Include enough details so that a reader will understand why it is special to you.*

Start Out

Use the questions below to help you get ideas. Add ideas of your own.

- What are some favorite things you own?

_____

_____

- Which of these objects would be the most interesting to describe? Why?

_____

_____

_____

_____

Now choose an object to write about. Write some details about the object that come to mind right away.

_____

_____

_____

_____

_____

_____

Read the details you listed. Then think about how you feel about this object. Why is it special to you? Write a sentence about what the object means to you. Use this sentence as your central idea.

_____

_____

_____

_____

Put It Together

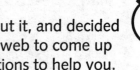

You've picked an object to describe, listed details about it, and decided on a central idea. Now you're ready to use the detail web to come up with details to use in your essay. Here are some questions to help you. You may add circles if you need to.

- What different kinds of things do I notice about my favorite object?
- What do I see when I look at it closely?
- Does it make any sounds? Does it have an odor or a taste?
- What does the object feel like to the touch?
- What are its characteristics that make it so special to me?

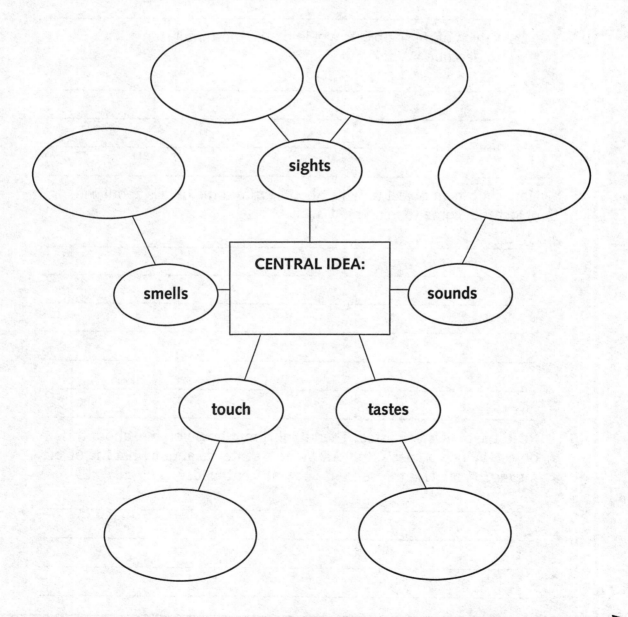

Write Your Essay

Use your detail web to write your descriptive essay.

Here are some ideas to think about.

- Remember to give the central idea in the first paragraph.
- Organize your details in groups that make sense together.
- Write about each group of details in a separate paragraph.
- End your descriptive essay with a closing paragraph that gives your central idea again.

Write your essay on a separate sheet of paper.

Look It Over

When you have finished writing, read your essay carefully. Then use this checklist to evaluate what you have written. Don't worry about spelling or grammar for now.

Circle a number on the scoring scale after each question. (**5** is the highest you can score; **1** is the lowest.)

Is the central idea clearly stated in the opening paragraph?

1 2 3 4 5

Does each paragraph tell about a group of details?

1 2 3 4 5

Do the details give a clear, complete picture of the object?

1 2 3 4 5

Does the essay end in an interesting way?

1 2 3 4 5

Think It Over

What did you think was the hardest part of writing this essay? What do you think could make it easier next time? Write your ideas on the lines below.

_____

_____

_____

_____

_____

4   How to Write an Expository Essay

Here's a prompt for an expository essay that might appear on a writing test.

> *Think of a useful invention. Write an essay explaining why you think the invention is useful.*

In order to write an expository essay for this prompt, select an item in an area that interests you. Then think of one or more reasons why the invention you've chosen is a useful one. One way to organize your thoughts before you begin writing the essay is to use a **topic chart**.

TOPIC:	The computer is a useful invention.
REASONS:	Computers are used in space travel. Some cars run by computer. Video games entertain people.
CONCLUSION:	Computers play a large part in today's world.

Compare the chart with these paragraphs from an expository essay.

It's hard to think of a more useful invention than the computer. Computers seem to be a part of almost everything we use.

If we didn't have computers, we could not have sent space-ships to the moon, Venus, and Mars. Computers run and direct these spaceships. They also allow the scientists on Earth to stay in contact with the spaceships.

Computers are used in almost all the cars being made today. In a new car, the computer controls nearly everything the engine does. If the computer fails, you can't even start your car.

Which reasons from the chart are used in the paragraph? What details did the writer add to each reason?

_____

_____

_____

Plan an Expository Essay

Now you plan an expository essay.

> *Think of something you couldn't do without. Write an essay explaining why this item makes your life easier or better.*

Start Out

Use these questions to help you get ideas. Add your own ideas.

- What are some things you use every day?

  _____

  _____

- Do any of these things improve your life?

  _____

  _____

- Imagine living without these things. Which one would you miss the most?

  _____

  _____

Choose one item to write about. Think about the reasons that this item is important to your life. Then jot down notes to use in your explanation.

_____ _____

_____

_____

_____

_____

_____

_____

_____

Read the details you listed. Use them to write a sentence that tells why the item is important. Use this sentence as your central idea.

_____

_____

_____

Put It Together

You've picked something to write about, listed reasons why it's important to you, and decided on a central idea. Now you're ready to fill in your chart. Here are some ideas to help you plan.

- Look back over the details you jotted down on the last page. You can probably use some of them in your chart.

- Remember to state why the item is important to you.

- List several reasons why you think this item makes your life easier or better.

- Come up with a conclusion that sums up the details and tells why the item is important to you. Be sure the final idea is an interesting one.

TOPIC:	_____
CENTRAL IDEA:	_____
REASONS:	_____
CONCLUSION:	_____

Write Your Essay

Use your chart to write your essay.

Here are some ideas to help you.

- Remember to give the central idea in the first paragraph.
- Write a paragraph for each reason that backs up your central idea.
- End the essay by giving your central idea in a fresh and interesting way.

Use a separate sheet of paper to write your essay.

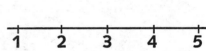
25 MIN

Look It Over

When you've finished writing, read your essay carefully. Use this checklist to evaluate what you've written. Don't worry about spelling or grammar for now.

Circle a number on the scoring scale to tell how you think you did. (**5** is the highest you can score; **1** is the lowest.)

Is the central idea clearly stated in the opening paragraph?

1   2   3   4   5

Do the other paragraphs tell about reasons why the item is important to you?

1   2   3   4   5

Have you clearly explained how this item helps you?

1   2   3   4   5

Will the closing paragraph help the reader remember the central idea?

1   2   3   4   5

Think It Over

What is one way that you could make your expository essay better? Write your ideas on the lines below.

_____

_____

_____

_____

_____

_____

_____

How to Write a Narrative Essay

Here's a prompt for a narrative essay that might appear on a writing test.

> *Think of a time when someone surprised you by doing something unexpected. Relate what happened during this experience.*

You can use a story map to plan a narrative essay. A **story map** shows each part of the story that the writer plans to tell about.

TOPIC:	Something I never expected
Central Idea:	Kevin proved I was wrong about him.
Details:	I thought Kevin was not my friend.
	Kids in class picked on me.
	Kevin stood up for me.
Conclusion:	It's easy to be wrong about people.

Compare the following paragraphs with the story map above.

Three months ago, Kevin was one of the people in my class I stayed away from. He never said anything friendly. I figured he just didn't like me. But Kevin proved I was wrong about him.

One day, some kids in the class decided I was their enemy. They started calling me names and making fun of everything I did. I tried to ignore them, but I kept getting angry.

Just when I was about to get into a fight, Kevin stepped in. He told them to leave me alone. He stood there, ready to back up his words. The other kids walked away and never bothered me again. Since then, Kevin has been one of my best friends.

The way Kevin stood up for me showed me that I was wrong about him. I guess it's pretty easy to be wrong about people.

Compare the essay and the story map. Circle the central idea sentence. Underline details that were mentioned on the story map.

Plan a Narrative Essay

Now you try planning a narrative essay.

> *Think of a time when you did something you didn't think you could do. Relate what happened during this experience.*

Start Out

Use the questions below to help you get ideas. Add your own ideas.

- What things do you have trouble doing?

  _____

  _____

- Have you ever surprised yourself by succeeding at one of these things?

  _____

  _____

  _____

  _____

Choose a topic for your story. Then jot down some notes about your experience.

WHERE _____

_____

WHEN _____

_____

WHAT HAPPENED _____

_____

_____

HOW I FELT _____

_____

_____

Now write a sentence that tells how you were able to do something you thought was impossible. Use this sentence as your central idea.

_____

_____

Put It Together

Now that you've picked something to write about, jotted down notes for your story, and decided on a central idea, you can use a story map to finish your plan. Here are some ideas to help you finish the map.

- Use the notes you made on the last page.
- Put the events in the order in which they happened.
- Use details to describe what happened and how you felt.
- Your conclusion should describe what you learned about yourself during this experience.

TOPIC: _____

_____

Central Idea: _____

_____

_____

_____

_____

_____

Details: _____

_____

_____

_____

_____

_____

Conclusion: _____

_____

_____

_____

Write Your Essay

Use your story map to write your essay. These ideas can help you.

- Remember to give the central idea in the first paragraph.
- In each supporting paragraph, use details to continue the story.
- In the closing paragraph, tell what you learned from your experience.

Use a separate sheet of paper for writing your essay.

Look It Over

When you've finished writing, read your essay carefully. Then use this checklist to evaluate what you have written. Don't worry about spelling or grammar for now.

Circle a number on the scoring scale after each question. (**5** is the highest you can score; **1** is the lowest.)

Is the central idea clearly stated in the opening paragraph?

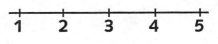
1 2 3 4 5

Did you tell the events in the order in which they happened?

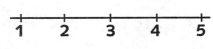
1 2 3 4 5

Does each supporting paragraph include more information about what happened?

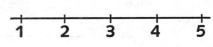
1 2 3 4 5

Does each supporting paragraph include details?

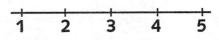
1 2 3 4 5

Does the closing paragraph return to the central idea?

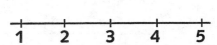
1 2 3 4 5

Think It Over

If you had to write this essay again, how would you change it? Write your ideas on the lines below.

_____

_____

_____

_____

_____

_____

Here's an outline of the topics in Unit 1. Jot down what is important about each point. These notes are just for you, so don't worry about writing complete sentences.

A. Parts of an Essay

1. Central Idea _____

_____

2. Introduction _____

_____

3. Body _____

_____

4. Closing _____

_____

B. Three Elements of Good Writing

1. Focus_____

_____

2. Support_____

_____

3. Organization _____

_____

C. Four Kinds of Essays

1. Persuasive_____

_____

2. Descriptive _____

_____

3. Expository_____

_____

4. Narrative_____

_____

UNIT 2

IMPROVING YOUR SCORE

What Can You Do to Be a Better Writer?

In Unit 1, you learned about four types of essays you may be asked to write on an essay test. In Unit 2, you will learn how to develop your ideas, write better sentences and paragraphs, and recognize and fix mistakes.

Remember that writing an essay is a **process**—a series of steps that leads to a finished product. If you follow all the steps in the process, your writing will improve. This picture can help you remember all the steps in the process.

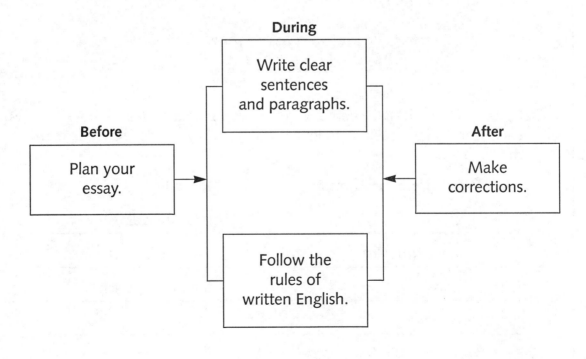

During

Write clear sentences and paragraphs.

Before

Plan your essay.

After

Make corrections.

Follow the rules of written English.

CHAPTER 1 PLANNING YOUR ESSAY

Careful planning can help you write a good essay. This chapter will show you how to **think** of ideas and how to **extend, focus,** and **organize** these ideas into an essay.

LESSON 1 How to Think of Ideas

"My mind used to go blank when I read a writing prompt. Now I know how to use the words in the prompt to get ideas. That's how I get started." —**Joseph Jackson, 15**

Try to feel relaxed and confident when you write. Remember, you have dozens of opinions, ideas, and feelings about all kinds of subjects. Begin by reading the prompt, such as the one below. Decide what type of essay you're being asked to write. Then look for key words in the prompt. What do these words mean to you?

> *Should schools spend more money on computers and new textbooks or on sports equipment and new uniforms? Write an essay in which you give your opinion.*

Start Out

Finding key words in a prompt can help you get ideas. Notice how each word below leads to an idea. Add other key words and ideas to the list below.

Key Words from the Prompt	Ideas
schools	educate kids
new textbooks	keep up-to-date
sports	teamwork, discipline
equipment	

Put It Together

Once you've gotten ideas from the key words in the prompt, you're ready to organize your ideas. Following these steps will help you.

1. Write your opinion in a sentence. This is your central idea.

2. Look at your list of key words and ideas. Which ideas support your central idea? Each will be a new paragraph in your essay.

3. Think of details to back up each of these supporting ideas.

Central Idea: _____

Supporting Idea: _____

Details: _____

_____

_____

Supporting Idea: _____

Details: _____

_____

_____

Write Your Essay

Use a separate sheet of paper to write your persuasive essay. Your goal is to give your opinion and to make your reader agree with it.

Look It Over

Reread your essay. Ask yourself these questions:

- Does my essay answer the prompt?
- Does each paragraph support my central idea?
- Do I use details to back up my ideas?
- Do I restate my central idea in the closing?

Think It Over

If you had to write this essay again, how would you change it?
Use the back of your essay to write your ideas.

How to Extend an Idea

"Sometimes when I read a prompt I can think of only one or two things to say. I don't know how to make a whole essay out of one or two ideas." —**Natasha Rivera, 16**

You may think that one or two ideas is not enough for a whole essay. But if each idea is **extended**, or filled out with information and details, it can be enough for an essay.

Here's a prompt that might appear on a writing test.

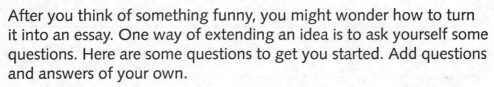

Think of something funny that happened to you or someone you know. Write an essay that tells how this incident taught you a lesson.

Start Out

After you think of something funny, you might wonder how to turn it into an essay. One way of extending an idea is to ask yourself some questions. Here are some questions to get you started. Add questions and answers of your own.

- **What** is the funny thing that happened?

  _____

- **Who** is involved in this event?

  _____

- **Where** did it take place?

  _____

- **When** did it take place?

  _____

- **Why** is it funny?

  _____

- **What** did you learn from what happened?

  _____

- _____

  _____

- _____

  _____

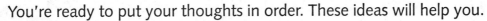

Put It Together

You're ready to put your thoughts in order. These ideas will help you.

1. What lesson does the story teach? Write the lesson in a sentence. Use this sentence as your central idea.

2. Give the events and actions in order as they took place. Each event or action will be a new main idea.

3. Fill out the events or actions with the details you listed.

Central Idea: _____

Main Idea: _____

Details: _____

_____

_____

Main Idea: _____

Details: _____

_____

_____

Write Your Essay

Write your narrative essay on a separate sheet of paper. Remember, your goal is to tell a funny story that teaches a lesson.

Look It Over

Reread your essay. Ask yourself these questions:

- Do the paragraphs tell the story in the order it happened?
- Do I use details to back up my ideas?
- Do I restate my central idea in the closing?

Think It Over

What was the hardest part of writing this essay? What would make it easier next time? Write your ideas on the back of your essay.

LESSON **3** **How to Focus Your Ideas**

"I read the prompt and had ideas to write about. But I didn't know where to start or when to stop." —**Karla Hayes, 15**

If you choose to write about something that is large or very familiar to you, you may have trouble deciding where to start and when to stop. Mapping out your ideas first can help you **focus** your ideas.

Here's a prompt that might appear on a writing test.

> *Describe one of your favorite places. Tell what you like about the place. Tell why it is your favorite place.*

Start Out

After you have a place in mind, think about its size. A place such as the state of Florida may be too large. You will need to **focus** your idea by picking a smaller place in the state—perhaps an amusement park, a beach, or a town.

A chart like the one below can help you decide which information to include and which to leave out. In each column, list at least two details. You may wish to form another category for other details.

Place you want to write about: _____		
What it looks like	**Things to do there**	
_____	_____	_____
_____	_____	_____
_____	_____	_____
_____	_____	_____
_____	_____	_____
_____	_____	_____
_____	_____	_____

Put It Together

Once you've focused your ideas, you're ready to put them in order.

1. Write a sentence that tells why you remember this place. You can use this sentence as your central idea.

2. Put the ideas you listed in your chart into paragraphs.

Central Idea: _____
What it looks like: _____   **Details:** _____   _____
Things to do there: _____   **Details:** _____   _____
Other category: _____   **Details:** _____   _____

Write Your Essay

Write your descriptive essay on a separate sheet of paper. Remember, your goal is to give the reader a clear idea of what you're describing.

Look It Over

Reread your essay. Ask yourself these questions:

- Do I give enough details?
- Do I restate my central idea in the closing?

Think It Over

Ask a friend to read your essay. Use your friend's reaction to tell how you would change your essay. Use the back of your essay to write your ideas.

How to Organize Information

"Sometimes I have a lot of information. Then it's hard to put it all together into an essay." —**Max Gomez, 16**

Here's a prompt you might see on a writing test.

> *Write an essay about how the television industry works. Organize the notes below and explain who profits when a TV program gets a big audience.*
> — *Company pays money to TV station for time slot to run commercials for its products*
> — *Producer of a program pays the costs of making program*
> — *Time slots during a program with a large audience are more expensive*
> — *TV station pays producer to show the program*
> — *Cost of program: writers, actors, director, camera operators, etc.*
> — *Company makes money when viewers see commercial and buy product*

Start Out

One way to organize facts is to group related facts together. Use the notes to complete the table below.

	Pays Money	**Makes Money**
Company	for time slot to show commercial during program	when people see commercial and buy product
TV Station	to show program	
Producer		

Put It Together

After your facts are grouped together, organize your essay.

Explain how each part of the TV industry pays and makes money. Write a paragraph for each. Remember to add a closing paragraph.

Central Idea: _____

Company: _____
Details: _____
_____
_____

TV Station: _____
Details: _____
_____
_____

Producer: _____
Details: _____
_____
_____

Write Your Essay

Write your expository essay on a separate sheet of paper. Remember, your goal is to explain information to the reader.

Look It Over

Reread your essay. Ask yourself these questions:

- Does each paragraph explain one part of the process?
- Do I use details to back up my ideas?
- Do I restate my central idea in the closing?

Think It Over

What do you think is the clearest explanation you gave in your essay? Explain why. Write your ideas on the back of your essay.

Put Your Learning into Practice

Think about what you have learned in the last four lessons. Then read the following four writing prompts. Choose an essay type that you have not done yet. Write your essay on a separate sheet of paper.

Persuasive

Think of a change that would improve your school cafeteria. Write an essay to convince your principal that this change should be made.

Narrative

Write an essay that tells a story about a time when you got into a disagreement with another student at your school. Tell what happened and what you learned from the experience.

Descriptive

Write an essay in which you describe a person you know and admire.

Expository

The notes below come from research on how the United States government is set up. Arrange and use these notes to write an essay. In the essay, explain how the structure of the government makes it impossible for any one person or group to gain too much power.

— The President is elected every four years.
— The Congress makes the laws.
— The Supreme Court may decide that a law is unconstitutional.
— Congressional representatives are elected every four years, and senators are elected every six years.
— The President may suggest laws to the Congress.
— Members of the Supreme Court are appointed by a President and may keep their jobs for the rest of their lives.

Start Out

- Use key words to help you think of ideas.
- Organize your thoughts before you write.

Put It Together

To plan your essay, use one of the methods you learned in this chapter. Before you write the essay, answer these questions:

- What is my central idea?
- What supporting ideas will I use in each of the paragraphs?
- What details will I use to support each idea in the essay?
- How will I restate my central idea in the closing?

 ## Write Your Essay

Write your essay on a separate sheet of paper. Remember the goal of the type of essay you are writing.

Look It Over

Check off things you have done to help you decide if you have written a successful essay.

Persuasive Essay

[ ]   Did you write your opinion of the change in the introduction?

[ ]   Did you develop your ideas with reasons, examples, and facts?

Narrative Essay

[ ]   Did you tell when and where events took place?

[ ]   Did you tell what you learned from the experience?

Descriptive Essay

[ ]   Did you use details to help the reader picture the person?

[ ]   Did you tell why you feel admiration for the person?

Expository Essay

[ ]   Did you put the notes in an order that makes sense?

[ ]   Did you leave out any of the notes that were provided?

 ## Think It Over

What is the hardest part of writing an essay? What can you do to make this easier next time? Write your response on a separate sheet of paper.

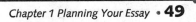

CHAPTER 2 — STRATEGIES FOR CLEAR AND INTERESTING WRITING

In this chapter, you will learn how to make your writing more interesting and easy to follow. You will learn to **connect** your ideas, **write** different kinds of sentences, and **organize** a paragraph. These skills will help you improve your score on the writing test.

LESSON 1 — How to Develop Good Transitions

A **transition** is a word or group of words that connects two ideas. Transitions can show the reader how two ideas are related. Look at the following list of transitions that you can use in your writing.

Check It Out

Transitions that show time order: *before, during, after, soon, next, then, finally, later, first, eventually, meanwhile*

Example:

   a. The weather this morning was delightful. **Later,** it became cloudy.

Transitions that show that ideas are similar: *also, in addition, furthermore, similarly, for example, for instance*

Example:

   b. This car needs a tune-up. **Also,** it could use a good wash!

Transitions that show that two ideas are not similar: *but, however, on the other hand, although, instead*

Example:

   c. The dog swam in the lake, **but** the cat stayed on the dry sand.

Transitions that show cause and effect: *because, as a result, for this reason, therefore*

Example:

   d. He studied hard. **As a result**, he got a good grade on the test.

Transitions that show physical position: *above, below, behind, nearby, in the distance, outside*

Example:

   e. The tree trunk did not move. **Above,** branches blew in the wind.

Work It Out

Each pair of sentences below could be linked with a transitional word or phrase. Fill in each blank with a transition that fits the meaning.

1. We waited a long time for the sun to set. _____, the sky filled with stars.

2. The little boy went to get help _____ the cat was stuck in the tree.

3. The room was very quiet. _____, I could hear birds singing.

4. I never knew my great-grandfather. _____, I've spent many hours looking at pictures of him.

5. A deer was taking a drink from a stream. _____, another deer sniffed the air.

6. This afternoon she exercised to keep in shape. _____, she warmed up her muscles so she wouldn't get hurt.

7. One of the painters used oils. _____, most of the other painters used watercolors.

8. Alfred Hitchcock movies are wonderful. _____, I love his movie *Vertigo*.

9. I practiced that dive many times. _____, I got it right.

10. That song makes me feel like dancing to the beat. _____, this song makes me feel quiet and sad.

11. The hot-air balloon flew by. _____, people stood in the field and cheered.

12. Jen decided not to go to the movies. _____, she watched a video at home.

13. The sky was cloudy in the morning. _____, the sun was shining by afternoon.

Look It Over

Reread the sentences. Can you think of other transitions to use in any of the sentences? Choose four sentences. On another sheet of paper, rewrite these sentences. This time use different transitions.

How to Combine Sentences

Combining, or joining, sentences will make your writing more interesting.

This is what sentences can be like when they are not combined:

I go to the park. I watch the kids play. I think about things.

Reading a whole essay of sentences like these would be uninteresting. That's because all three sentences sound similar and are the same length.

By combining sentences, you can make your writing sound more natural:

I go to the park to watch the kids play. I think about things.

When combining sentences, try to write a mixture of sentences that look and sound different from one another.

Check It Out

Here are some ways to combine sentences in writing.

Combine names of persons or things.

Example:

    a. Marla takes dancing lessons. Fred takes dancing lessons.

Correction:

    b. Marla and Fred take dancing lessons.

Combine action words.

Example:

    c. The car stalled. It would not start for five minutes.

Correction:

    d. The car **stalled and would not start** for five minutes.

Combine whole sentences by using a transition word.

Example:

    e. Beth wants to get a job. She can work only two days a week.

Correction:

    f. Beth wants to get a job, **but** she can work only two days a week.

Put information from one sentence into another sentence.

Example:

    g. The green house belongs to my aunt. It is near the train station.

Correction:

    h. The green house **near the train station** belongs to my aunt.

Work It Out

Rewrite each pair of sentences as a single sentence. Try to use each of the four methods on the opposite page at least once.

1. Sandra stepped up to the foul line. She scored the winning basket.

    _____

    _____

2. He saw a squirrel hiding from the cat. The squirrel was behind a bush.

    _____

    _____

3. Nicole told a joke to the class. Everybody laughed.

    _____

    _____

4. Jorge bought tickets to the play. Carla bought tickets to the play.

    _____

    _____

5. I had a surprise for my little sister. It was in the shopping bag.

    _____

    _____

6. We showed ID cards to the teacher. We walked into the assembly hall.

    _____

    _____

7. Frank is a reporter on the school paper. He is the best writer in the class.

    _____

    _____

Look It Over

Look over the sentence pairs again. Find one pair that could be combined in a different way. Write the new sentence on a separate sheet of paper.

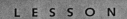

How to Structure a Paragraph

In an essay, you present your thoughts in order. When you write a paragraph, you do exactly the same thing. In each paragraph, write the main idea in a **topic sentence**. In the sentences that follow, give **supporting details**. These details can be reasons, examples, and facts that support the main idea. Structuring your paragraphs this way will make your writing clearer.

Check It Out

You can improve the structure of a paragraph by following these steps:

1. Choose a single idea for a paragraph.

2. Begin a paragraph with a topic sentence that states a main idea.

3. Use the rest of the paragraph to give details supporting this main idea.

4. In the last sentence of the paragraph, state the main idea in a different way.

Here is a paragraph with good structure:

> Some people will do anything to look good—even if it is bad   1
> for them. I know a person who ate nothing but one grapefruit a   2
> day until she fainted right in the middle of a gym class. Another   3
> person I know worked out all the time because he wanted big   4
> muscles. He hurt his back lifting weights. Even a famous   5
> celebrity said that she used to sleep with a clothes pin on her   6
> nose to try and change the shape of her nose. Of course, it didn't   7
> work and only made her nose sore. Everybody wants to look   8
> good, but it's more important to feel good about yourself.   9

- The topic sentence is stated in line 1. It states the main idea of the paragraph: Some people do harmful things to themselves to try to look good.

- The entire paragraph is about the single idea that some people will do anything to look good.

- Sentences 2-8 tell more about this idea. They support the idea with details and examples.

- The last sentence on lines 8 and 9 restates the main idea in a different way.

Work It Out

Read each paragraph. Look at the letters before each sentence. Then answer the questions that follow by circling the correct letter or letters.

A.   **(a)** Of all the days of the week, I think Fridays are the best.

   (b) Monday morning is a rude awakening after the weekend.

   (c) Tuesday doesn't seem much different. **(d)** By Thursday,

   the weekend has come into sight. **(e)** But there's nothing like

   Friday, my favorite day of the week.

   1. Which sentence is the main idea?   (a) (b) (c) (d) (e)

   2. Which sentences support this idea?   (a) (b) (c) (d) (e)

   3. Which sentence restates the main idea?   (a) (b) (c) (d) (e)

B.   **(a)** Caring for plants can be tricky. **(b)** I used to think that plants

   needed only a little water once a week and a sunny spot near a

   window. **(c)** But I've seen plants grow better when I let them dry

   out. **(d)** One plant grew like crazy when I moved it out of the sun.

   (e) Caring for plants isn't always easy, but it's worth it.

   1. Which sentence is the main idea?   (a) (b) (c) (d) (e)

   2. Which sentences support this idea?   (a) (b) (c) (d) (e)

   3. Which sentence restates the main idea?   (a) (b) (c) (d) (e)

Look It Over

Add a sentence to the first paragraph that you think will make it better. Write your sentence on the lines below.

_____

_____

_____

_____

_____

_____

Put Your Learning into Practice

Read the following writing prompts. Think about what you have learned about using transitions, combining sentences, and structuring paragraphs. Use what you have learned to write an essay. Write a different type of essay than the one you wrote at the end of Chapter 1.

Persuasive

Imagine that the local school board plans to cut all after-school activities in order to save money. Decide which activities should not be cut. Write an essay in which you try to persuade the school board of your opinion.

Descriptive

Write a description of something that you would like to own.

Expository

What advice would you give to a tourist or visitor to your town or city? Write an essay in which you give interesting and helpful information about the place where you live.

Narrative

Imagine that you have become a new kind of superhero. Write an essay that tells your story. Use a separate paragraph for each part of your story—for example, what your birth and childhood were like, how you got your powers, and what your present life is like.

Start Out

5 MIN

Write a sentence that states your central idea. If you have trouble finding an idea, remember to look for key words in the prompt. You may wish to use a separate sheet of paper to make a chart, a story map, or a web to organize your ideas.

_____

_____

_____

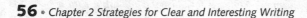

Put It Together

After listing and organizing your ideas, write at least two sentences that support your central idea. Use each as the main idea of one paragraph.

Main idea 1: _____

_____

Main idea 2: _____

_____

Write Your Essay

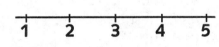

Write your essay on a separate sheet of paper. As you write, remember what you've learned about transitions, combining sentences, and structuring paragraphs.

Look It Over

When you've finished writing, read your essay carefully. Then use the following checklist to evaluate what you have written. Don't worry about spelling or grammar for now.

Circle a number on the scoring scale after each question. (**5** is the highest you can score; **1** is the lowest.)

How well do you answer the question or topic in the prompt?	1 2 3 4 5
Does each paragraph in the body contain an idea and supporting details?	1 2 3 4 5
Does your closing paragraph restate the central idea?	1 2 3 4 5
How well do you use transitions to connect ideas?	1 2 3 4 5
How well were you able to combine sentences?	1 2 3 4 5

Think It Over

What do you think is the best part of your essay? What part of your essay do you think needs more work? Write what you think on the back of your essay. Explain the reasons for your choices.

CHAPTER 3 — MECHANICS AND USAGE

This chapter gives you some basic rules for writing. On writing tests, you'll be graded on how well you have followed these rules.

LESSON 1 — Sentence Structure

A sentence has a **subject** and a **verb**. The subject names the person, place, thing, or idea the sentence is about. The verb tells what the subject is or does.

Check It Out

Here are some rules for writing a sentence.

A sentence must express a complete thought.

Examples:

   a. **Fred walked.**

Fred is the subject. Walked is the verb. It tells what Fred did.

   b. **Fred is healthy.**   c. **Fred has strong muscles.**

Verbs such as *to be* (*is, am, are, was, were*) and *to have* (*has, have, had*) must be followed by one or more other words to complete the thought.

The subject does not always begin a sentence. The subject is not always followed directly by the verb.

Example:

   d. **The house with the two chimneys was my favorite.**

Subjects and verbs can be singular or plural.

Singular		Plural	
Subject	Verb	Subject	Verb
jacket	looks	jackets	look

A singular subject takes a singular verb. A plural subject takes a plural verb. This is called subject-verb agreement.

Examples:

   e. **The jacket looks great.**
   f. **The jackets look great.**

Work It Out

Read each sentence below. Then underline the subject once and the correct verb in parentheses twice.

1. My older brother (wants, want) his own apartment.

2. José already (has, have) a full-time job at a bookstore.

3. My mother and I (thinks, think) that he should wait until next year to move.

4. My grandparents (is visiting, are visiting) us for two weeks this summer.

5. They (agrees, agree) with my brother about his getting an apartment.

6. José and a friend (is planning, are planning) to share the cost of the apartment.

7. Living on your own (costs, cost) a lot of money these days.

8. Most kids my age (enjoys, enjoy) living at home.

9. My parents (promises, promise) that I'll get José's room after he moves into his apartment.

Look It Over

Which sentence was the most difficult for you to fix? How did you decide what to do?

_____

_____

_____

_____

_____

_____

Sentence Fragments and Run-On Sentences

A sentence must express a complete thought and have a subject and verb.

Check It Out

Sentence fragments are usually missing a subject or a verb.

Examples:

   a. Forgot my book. (no subject)

   b. Bill and Joan. (no verb)

Sentence fragments can be corrected by giving the missing subject or verb and adding information.

Corrections:

   c. I forgot my book.   **d.** Bill and Joan **found the book.**

Sentence fragments can have a subject and a verb, but still not express a complete thought.

Example:

   e. Or I left it at home. (subject and verb but no complete thought)

Sentence fragments can be corrected by completing the thought.

Correction:

   f. **Either I left the book in school,** or I left it at home.

Run-on sentences join two or more sentences incorrectly.

Example:

   g. We left our jackets at home, we didn't need them because it was so hot.

Run-on sentences can be corrected by writing two sentences.

Correction:

   h. We left our jackets at **home. We** didn't need them because it was so hot.

Example:

   i. The two of us sat in the sun most of the afternoon, we got terrible sunburns.

Run-on sentences can be corrected by using transition words to show how ideas are connected.

Correction:

   j. **Because** the two of us sat in the sun most of the afternoon, we got terrible sunburns.

Work It Out

Each of these items is a run-on sentence or a sentence fragment. On the lines below each one, rewrite the item correctly as one or two complete sentences.

1. I like this music it makes me want to dance.

_____

_____

2. Took the time to do the job right.

_____

_____

3. Crowded into the lunch room just after the bell.

_____

_____

4. I like that class, the teacher always tells us interesting things.

_____

_____

5. She played the piano, I played the guitar.

_____

_____

6. A narrow road up the side of the mountain.

_____

_____

7. An expert on all kinds of cars.

_____

_____

Look It Over

Look back at your work. Are there any sentences that you could have corrected in a different way? On a separate sheet of paper, write these new corrections. Then decide which correction you think works best.

Adjectives and Adverbs

Using adjectives and adverbs will make your writing more detailed and interesting.

Check It Out

An adjective describes a noun or a pronoun.

Adjectives answer these questions about nouns and pronouns: *Which one? Whose is it? What kind? How many?*

Example:

    a. The **tired, hungry** marchers slept on the grass when the parade was over.

The adjectives *tired* and *hungry* tell what kind of marchers.

An adverb describes a verb, an adjective, or another adverb.

Adverbs answer these questions about verbs, adjectives, or other adverbs: *How? Where? When? How much?*

Examples:

    b. The people went **downstairs** after lunch.

The adverb *downstairs* describes the verb *went*. It tells where the people went.

    c. The man looked **up** and saw a **mostly** blue sky.

The adverb *up* tells where the man looked. The adverb *mostly* describes the adjective *blue*. It tells how much of the sky was blue.

    d. Because of the rain, all the planes arrived **extremely late**.

The adverb *late* describes the verb *arrived*; it tells when the planes arrived. The adverb *extremely* describes the adverb *late*; it tells how much the planes were *late*.

You can use adjectives to compare people or things.

Examples:

    e. This test is **harder** than the one we took last week.

    f. This is the **hardest** test I've ever taken.

The ending *-er* is added to the adjective *hard* to compare two tests. The ending *-est* is added to *hard* to compare more than two tests.

With longer adjectives such as *confident,* use the adjective with an adverb such as *more, most,* or *less.*

Example:

    g. Tama is **more confident** than Chris about winning the game.

Work It Out

In the following sentences, circle the adjectives and write adv above the adverbs.

1. The party was fun, but Scott yawned repeatedly.

2. He needed to sleep to prepare for the big game.

3. Yesterday the coach finally decided that Scott could play.

4. Scott was nervous because he wanted to do well.

5. He is the most dedicated player on the team.

6. The day of the game was sunny and beautiful.

7. Scott ate a good breakfast.

8. He walked quickly from his house to the empty field.

9. The hours soon passed, and the important game began.

10. During the game, he caught a long pass.

11. The coach said, "Good job, Scott!"

12. When Scott relaxed, he played better than the other players.

13. Scott's proud family cheered loudly.

14. Scott became a much more confident player.

Look It Over

Look over your work on adjectives and adverbs. Choose two adjectives and two adverbs. On a separate sheet of paper, use them in sentences of your own.

Capitalization and End Punctuation

You probably recognize capital letters and punctuation marks that end sentences. Here are some rules to help you use both correctly.

Check It Out

Use a capital letter at the beginning of a sentence.

Example:

    a. The senior class performed a play for the school.

Use capital letters for the days of the week, months, and holidays.

Examples:

    b. Saturday, July, Independence Day

Use a capital letter at the beginning of a direct quotation in dialogue.

Example:

    c. She asked, "Are you going to take the test tomorrow?"

    d. "Here on this ledge," the man said, "is where I found it."

If a quotation is broken up, only capitalize the beginning part.

Use a capital letter for the names of particular people, places, or things (including titles, languages, organizations, and events).

Examples:

    e. Frank Sinatra, Sears Tower, Los Angeles, President Clinton

    f. Missouri River, the Civil War, National Football League

Use a capital letter for the first and last word and the main words in the title of a book, movie, play, or long poem.

Example:

    g. *The Catcher in the Rye*, *The Phantom of the Opera*

Here are some basic rules of punctuation:

- **End statements with a period.**

- **End questions with a question mark.**

- **End exclamations of emotion or surprise with an exclamation point.**

Examples:

    h. The rain lasted over two weeks.

    i. What have you done with my straw hat?

    j. Wow! That movie was great!

Work It Out

For each of the following sentences, add correct end punctuation and underline the letters that should be capitalized

1. Kim got good grades in science and spanish

2. They met at Shea Boulevard and Market street

3. The guest speaker was reverend Atkinson

4. How close is the grand canyon to Mexico

5. She is reading a biography of mary todd lincoln

6. My uncle lives on the coast of florida

7. Patrick Henry spoke the famous quote, "give me liberty or give me death"

8. I'm so sleepy i can hardly talk

9. This birthday gift is from aunt Laura

10. Can i help you wash the car

11. Do the people in Austria speak german

12. Her cousin became an american citizen last month

13. The family decided to spend columbus day at crystal lake

14. last summer I read a book called native son

Look It Over

Look over the sentences you just corrected. On a separate sheet of paper, write the capitalization rule that is hardest for you to remember. Then find an example in which you correctly followed the rule.

Commas

Remember the rules for using commas when writing your essays.

Check It Out

Commas are used to separate items in a series.

Examples:

   a. They painted the **walls,** the **ceiling,** and the **door.**

   b. Ask **Laura, Jamal,** and **Martha** to help you.

Commas are used before the connecting words (such as *and, or, but,* **and** *though***) that join two sentences.**

Examples:

   c. The basketball fell through the hoop, **and** the crowd cheered.

   d. Wait for us at the bus stop, **or** meet us at school.

Commas are used to set off extra information that interrupts a sentence.

Example:

   e. Mark Twain, **the author of *Roughing It*,** died in 1910.

Commas are used to set off someone's exact words from the other words in a sentence.

Examples:

   f. Wilma asked, **"Who remembered to bring the mustard?"**

   g. **"I did,"** Alan answered.

Commas are used to separate the day and the year in a date.

Example:

   h. On **April 18, 1972,** I moved from Haiti to the United States.

Commas are used to set off the city and the state in a sentence.

Example:

   i. When we moved to **Atlanta, Georgia,** my mother got a new job.

Commas are used to set off some introductory words or phrases.

Examples:

   j. **No,** I'm afraid I can't join you.

   k. **After the fireworks,** we walked all the way around the lake.

Commas are used to set off a name used in direct address.

Example:

   l. Can I borrow your bike, **Michael?**

Work It Out

Each sentence below needs one or more commas. Add commas wherever they are needed.

1. We wanted to watch that program but the television broke.

2. Walter Stanton the tallest boy in our class hates basketball.

3. After the class was quiet the teacher gave the assignment.

4. "My cousin lives in Billings Montana" he explained.

5. My mother was born on July 17 1956 in Thailand.

6. I need two hard-boiled eggs for the experiment Mike.

7. Is Miami Florida larger than Boston Massachusetts?

8. The Mississippi River is the longest river in the United States but it is not as long as the Nile River.

9. Our school does well in baseball football and soccer.

10. "I like the art on the cover of that book" Jorge said.

11. Monica Ortiz my cousin from Mexico is coming to visit us.

12. The store sells comic books videos posters records and candy.

13. Yes I know that I have not used the diving board.

14. What does the date March 4 1959 mean to you?

Look It Over

Look over the sentences you just corrected. Which rule for commas gave you the most trouble? Write the rule on a separate sheet of paper. Then write one of the sentences from this exercise that shows how the rule is used correctly.

Semicolons and Quotation Marks

The person who grades your test will take off points for errors in punctuation. This lesson will help you use semicolons and quotation marks correctly.

Check It Out

Use a semicolon to connect two closely-related sentences that do not have a connecting word.

Examples:

   a. Vicky performed a dance for the talent show**;** Tim sang.

   b. The skater fell to the ice**;** she sprained her left ankle.

Use a semicolon before the words *however, for example, therefore,* **and** *nevertheless* **when they are used to connect two sentences.**

Examples:

   c. I hope to become a carpenter**; however,** my father wants me to be an electrician.

   d. Jane lives in Chicago**; therefore,** she is familiar with Lake Michigan.

   e. Carlos fell on the third lap**; nevertheless,** he won the race.

Use a semicolon to separate items in a series that include commas.

Example:

   f. The rehearsals are scheduled for **Monday, January 12; Wednesday, January 21;** and **Friday, January 23**.

Use quotation marks around someone's exact words.

Examples:

   g. Olivia said, **"I think I'll go home now."**

   h. **"I want to know,"** he repeated, **"why you didn't call me."**

Use quotation marks around the titles of songs, poems, short stories, and speeches.

Examples:

   i. I will never forget Martin Luther King's **"I Have a Dream"** speech.

   j. **"We are the World"** was popular in 1984.

   k. **"A Fine Day for Bananafish"** is one of my favorite short stories.

   l. **"Hold Fast Your Dreams"** by Louise Driscoll is a wonderful poem.

Work It Out

Each sentence below is missing either a semicolon or quotation marks.
Add the correct punctuation to each sentence.

1. The snowstorm is moving east quickly therefore it is expected to arrive in the city by noon.

2. Where, Cassie asked, can I find a map of South America?

3. Shawn said, I don't know anybody who owns a computer.

4. Have you studied the poem The Raven yet?

5. We waved goodbye the bus pulled away from the station.

6. Is this the best place, he asked, to hang this picture?

7. The show went on tour to Raleigh, North Carolina Memphis, Tennessee and Austin, Texas.

8. We knew we needed to hurry the store closes exactly at six o'clock.

9. I wrote a short story called The Unopened Box.

10. The clerk said, This model just happens to be on sale.

11. Boris asked, Has anyone seen my green hat?

12. I can't let any more riders on this bus, said the driver.

13. I wasn't crazy about the movie however, I must say that the hero reminded me of myself.

Look It Over

Review your work. Which rules for semicolons and quotation marks gave you trouble? Give yourself more practice by writing a sample sentence for each of these rules.

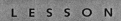 **Apostrophes**

This lesson will teach you how to use the apostrophe (') correctly.

Check It Out

An apostrophe is used in a contraction to show letters are missing.

Example:

  a. They didn't know.

The apostrophe replaces the *o* in *not.* **Did not = didn't.**

An apostrophe is used in possessives to show ownership.

Examples:

  b. This is David**'s** bike.

The *'s* shows that the bike belongs to David.

  c. The students**'** haircuts are completely different.

The *s* at the end of *students* means that there is more than one student. The apostrophe means that the haircuts belong to the students.

  d. The reporters listened to the editor-in-chief**'s** speech.

Add an *'s* to hyphenated words such as *editor-in-chief.*

  e. The husband**'s** and wife**'s** towels hung in the bathroom.

Use *'s* with both words to show separate ownership.

An apostrophe is used in some plurals to show there is more than one of something.

Example:

  f. I got three **B's** and two **A's** on my report card.

Use apostrophes for plurals of letters, numbers, and symbols.

Do not use apostrophes in the possessive pronouns *its, his, hers, yours, theirs,* **and** *ours.*

Examples:

  g. The dog hurt **its** leg.   **h.** This book is **yours**.

Do not use apostrophes with plurals that are not possessive.

Example:

  i. The **awards** were given to **performers** in **plays** all over the nation.

Do not confuse words that sound the same.

Examples:

  j. They're coming to get **their** prizes.

They're is a contraction of *they are. Their* is a possessive pronoun.

Work It Out

Each of the following sentences contains one mistake involving apostrophes. You may need to add an apostrophe or take one out Change any incorrect words you find.

1. The party is at Michaels house tonight.

2. This isnt the shortest way to get to the park.

3. His two sisters cars were parked in the driveway.

4. These flowers are her's.

5. This is the author's third book, and I bet its a good mystery.

6. It's ending is really going to surprise you.

7. Hasnt anyone ever shown you how to juggle three oranges?

8. Is his sister-in-laws apartment in town?

9. Whose going to take care of the children tonight?

10. Who's pen did you find under that desk?

11. Ive taken six train trips in the last two years.

12. The plants arent going to grow without some sunlight.

13. Theyre planning a class trip to the Blue Ridge Mountains.

14. He decided to save the book, even though it's pages were torn.

15. All my friends parents are strict.

Look It Over

Choose three of the sentences you just corrected. On a separate sheet of paper, write the number of each sentence and the rule you used to correct it.

Spelling Hints

The best way to improve your spelling is to keep a list of words that give you trouble. Look up each word, say it aloud, and write it in one or two sentences. Remember, good spelling takes practice.

Check It Out

Here are a few spelling rules that you should know:

Usually place *i* before *e* except after *c*.

Examples:

   a. My **friend** believes she can be fire **chief** one day.

   b. They got a **receipt** for the new **ceiling**.

An exception to this rule happens when the letters *ei* are sounded as if to rhyme with *day.*

Example:

   c. My **neighbor's** cat **weighs** a lot.

Make most nouns plural by adding the letter *s*.
However: If a noun ends in *s, x, z, ch, or sh*, then make it plural by adding the letters *es.*

Examples:

   d. bus/buses, fox/foxes, buzz/buzzes, church/churches, wish/wishes

If a noun ends in a consonant and the letter *y*, drop the *y* and add *ies* to form the plural.

Examples:

   e. city/cities, party/parties, baby/babies

If a noun ends in a vowel and the letter *y*, add the letter *s* to form the plural.

Examples:

   f. day/days, key/keys, monkey/monkeys, toy/toys

Here are a few hints to help you remember the differences between words that sound the same but have different spellings.

To remember the difference between *principal* and *principle*, remember these two sentences:

     Would you like the princi**pal** to be your **pal**?

     A princip**le** is a ru**le** to live by.

To remember the difference between *stationary* and *stationery*, remember these two sentences:

     You can buy writing pap**er** in a station**ery** store.

     A **car** is not very useful if it's station**ar**y.

Work It Out

Most of these sentences contain a misspelled word. If you find a word that is misspelled, rewrite the word correctly on the line that follows the sentence. If there are no misspelled words in that sentence, write "Correct" on that line.

1. Two different jurys have found him innocent. _____

2. I don't know what to believe. _____

3. They've painted all the benchs in the park. _____

4. Did they recieve a notice in the mail? _____

5. Stationary means standing still. _____

6. Do they sell stationary in that store? _____

7. Who is the principle of your school? _____

8. The children wanted to ride on the donkies. _____

9. They wanted to ride on the ponys, too. _____

10. They were releived when the ride was over. _____

11. We couldn't wait to open the boxs. _____

12. He was handsome but very conceited. _____

13. The monkies in the zoo look very sad. _____

14. There are not enough bus's running
    on weekends. _____

Look It Over

Make a list of words that you have had trouble spelling. On a separate sheet of paper, practice spelling these words by writing a sentence for each one.

Put Your Learning Into Practice

Read the four writing prompts below. Choose one that you would like to write an essay about. Pick a type of essay that is different from the type you chose at the end of Chapters 1 and 2. As you write and look over your essay, try to use what you have learned in this chapter about sentence structure, capitalization, punctuation, and spelling.

Persuasive

Imagine that your school has begun a recycling program and is publishing a newsletter that explains why people should take part. Write an essay for the newsletter in which you explain why recycling newspapers and other items is a good idea.

Descriptive

Write a description of a place you have enjoyed visiting or a place that you found scary. Tell why you liked the place or were scared by it.

Expository

In high school, most students begin to take on more and more responsibilities—both in school and out of school. Write an essay explaining what kinds of responsibilities some teenagers have.

Narrative

Write a narrative essay about some adventure or interesting thing that happened to you as a young child. Why was the event meaningful to you?

Start Out

Jot down some ideas about the prompt you chose. Use those ideas to come up with a central idea sentence.

_____

_____

_____

Put It Together

Here are some questions to think about before you write your essay.

- Are you sure your central idea statement answers the prompt?
- Do you have enough details about your central idea?
- Will you have a strong conclusion?

Write Your Essay

Write your essay on a separate sheet of paper. Use your notes to help you.

Look It Over

When your essay is finished, read it over carefully. Then use this checklist to find out how you can improve it.

Circle a number on the scoring scale to tell how you think you did. (**5** is the highest you can score; **1** is the lowest.)

Is the central idea stated in the first paragraph?	1 2 3 4 5
Does each body paragraph have a main idea and supporting details?	1 2 3 4 5
Is the information in the essay organized clearly?	1 2 3 4 5
Is the central idea restated in the last paragraph?	1 2 3 4 5
Does each sentence express a complete thought?	1 2 3 4 5
Does each sentence begin with a capital letter?	1 2 3 4 5
Does each sentence end with correct punctuation?	1 2 3 4 5
Does the essay contain any spelling errors?	1 2 3 4 5

Think It Over

Suppose you could make one change in your essay to improve it. What would it be? Write your ideas on the back of your essay.

CHAPTER 4 REVISING AND PROOFREADING

The writing of an essay is only part of the job. On the test, you'll also need to revise it. When you revise, you change what you've written to make it better. This chapter will show you how to revise your essay.

LESSON 1 Recognize Mistakes

The first step in revising mistakes is to find the mistakes. These guidelines will help you.

Check It Out

Use this list of main points to look for when you revise.

1. **Does each paragraph do what it's supposed to do?**
   The opening paragraph should state the central idea. The paragraphs in the body should support the central idea. The closing paragraph should restate the main thoughts and the central idea.

2. **Will a reader be able to follow the essay?**
   Be sure the ideas are laid out in logical order. Use transitional words to lead the reader clearly from one thought to another. Be sure the paragraphs are ordered correctly.

3. **Does the essay correctly answer the prompt?**
   Be sure the essay clearly covers what the prompt asks for. Cross out information that doesn't belong.

4. **Does each sentence have a subject and a verb?**
   Make sure there are no sentence fragments. Each sentence should express a complete thought.

5. **Do subjects and verbs agree—singular subjects with singular verbs, plural subjects with plural verbs?**
   Incorrect agreement between subjects and verbs makes writing confusing to read. Correct agreement states ideas clearly.

6. **Are sentences punctuated correctly, avoiding run-on sentences?**
Run-on sentences confuse readers. The simplest way to correct run-ons is to break them into separate sentences, each expressing a complete idea.

7. **Are there any sentences that could be combined?**
Combining sentences can help avoid repetition, make writing smoother, and focus ideas.

8. **Are capitalization, punctuation, and spelling correct?**
Proofreading for correct usage and spelling is important for turning out a polished final version of an essay.

The most important thing to keep in mind as you read your own writing is focus. If writing stays focused, concentrating on only the central idea and its supporting details, it will be good writing.

Read the following student paragraph. Underline parts of the paragraph that need correction. Think about the kind of correction needed in each case. Remember that sometimes there is more than one way to correct an error. Then look at the corrected version of the paragraph. Did you identify each error correctly?

Draft

Televison programs are much to violent. just for two or three hours. Youll probably see a few murders. You'll also probably see a couple of beatings. The other thing about television is that there are too many comercials. Young people who watch too many of these violent shows may start to think its alright to beat people or even kill them.

Corrected Version

Television programs are much too violent. Watch television for just two or three hours. You'll probably see a couple of beatings and a few murders. Young people who watch too many of these violent shows may start to think it's all right to beat people or even kill them.

Work It Out

Read each paragraph below, and think about how you could improve it. Review the list of points to look for when you revise. Underline each place where you think a correction is needed. Then write a revised version of each paragraph on the lines provided.

1. Using public transportation has advantages over driving privit cars. If more people used buses and tranes, fewer cars would be one the streets. Less air pollution! There would be less noise, to. Fewer cars would also mean fewer acidents. people should use public transportation when they can.

_____

_____

_____

_____

_____

_____

2. Making a salad is easy any one can do it. Salads are good for you, too. First you need to get some vegetables from the refrigerator. Lettuce, tomatoes, cucumbers, carets, and onions makes a great salad! Wash all the vegetables. tear the lettice into little peaces. Cut the other vegetables. Put everything in a bowl. Some salad dressing. Now youre ready to eat.

_____

_____

_____

_____

_____

_____

3. Success to me means being happy. Some people think that success means having things like a cool car and a big house. Their are people who have these things, they still arent happy. So how can success be having these things. Plenty of people who live in a small apartment and drive an old car is happy. My aunt's house near a shopping center. If you are looking for success, you should ask yourself, What makes me happy?

_____

_____

_____

_____

_____

_____

_____

_____

_____

_____

_____

_____

Look It Over

Reread one of the paragraphs you just revised. Then review the list of important points at the beginning of this chapter. Did you forget to check anything? Write a reminder to yourself that will help you to remember whatever you forgot to check for.

_____

_____

_____

_____

_____

_____

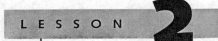
Decide Which Mistakes You Have Time to Fix

During a writing test, you need to plan, write, and revise your essay. Remember to leave time for revising and proofreading.

Check It Out

Plan to leave yourself 10 minutes at the end of a writing test to revise and proofread your essay. Even that may not be enough time to make all the changes that you want to make. That's why you should decide which changes you should make first.

Here is a checklist of questions to ask yourself as you revise. You don't have to memorize the list word-for-word, but keeping its points in mind will help you find other mistakes.

- Does my essay cover everything the prompt asked for?

- Is everything in my essay related to my central idea?

- Have I included facts, examples, and reasons that support what I say?

- Are my ideas in logical order and easy to follow?

- Do my paragraphs flow smoothly?

- Do I use transitions to move from one idea to another?

- Have I combined sentences where I could?

- Do I have any sentence fragments or run-on sentences?

- Have I used adjectives and adverbs correctly?

- Have I used capitalization and punctuation correctly?

When you read your essay, try to correct any mistakes you see as quickly as possible. If you don't see any mistakes, ask yourself the questions on this list. They will help you find mistakes that you might not see right away.

Which of the mistakes listed above are you most likely and least likely to make? Write your ideas below.

_____

_____

_____

_____

Work It Out

Read the following prompt and essay. Underline anything in the essay you think should be changed. Identify and number the three or four points you think are most important to fix. Rewrite the essay on a separate sheet of paper. Before you begin reading, note the time. See how much time you take to read and revise the essay.

> *Does your school have a rule or a code with which you strongly agree or disagree? State the rule or code, and why you agree or disagree with it.*

My school has a rule against personal stereos. I think the rule should be dropped. We should be able to listen to music. Then we would be better students. The school would be a better place to be.

I like to listen to music all the time. a free country, I have the right to do what I want.

Music makes people study better. I listen to music while I do my homework, all my friends do, too. If we don't listen to music. We can't concentrate. Having personal stereos in school would make us better students.

Music makes people happy. Listening to music makes everyone feel good. If we could wear headsets in school, we'd look forward to coming to school.

I agree that we shouldn't wear headsets when a teacher is talking to us, but we could read while hearing music. We could eat lunch to music. We would live better with music.

Look It Over

How did you decide which three or four points were the most important to correct in the essay?

_____

_____

_____

_____

_____

_____

_____

Put Your Learning into Practice

Now you know what to look for when you revise and proofread an essay. You have also decided which points are the most important to fix. All you need now is practice in revising and proofreading.

Check It Out

You can use what you've learned in this chapter to revise many kinds of writing.

Work It Out

Read this prompt and essay, and underline places where you would make changes. Then rewrite the essay correctly on page 83.

> Tell about an event that happened some time ago and that taught you a lesson.

The first time I rode a ten-speed bike was a few years ago. I really learned something from that ride. I learned that sometimes I dont know as much as I think I do.

The bike belonged to my next-door neighbor. His name is Dave, he's three years older than I am. Dave said my bike was a baby bike. It had no gears. It had these big, fat tires. He said it was time for me to move up to a grown-up bike. I said, "I can ride any bike as long as I can reach the pedals."

Dave did three things to get me ready. First, he lowered the seat. He showed me how to work the gears. Finally, he adjusted the straps on his helmet. To make it fit on my head. I was annoyed. I just wanted to get on that bike and ride.

Dave gave me one last warning. "It isnt going to feel like your bike, he said. "Take it easy at first." I knew better. How different could this bike be from mine?

It turned out to be very difrent. It had really narrow tires. That made it hard to keep my balance. It also moved faster than my bike. It had hand brakes. Instead of a pedal break.

At first, I tried to brake with the pedals. That didn't work. Then I squeezed on the hand brakes. I stopped short. The bike tipped over. I was flat on the ground.

Dave ran up to me. He was laughing. "I told you this is a different kind of bike," he said. He was right. I tried the bike again. This time, I was careful not to go too fast.

I learned something from that ride. Its okay to be confident, but you can be too confident for your own good.

Rewrite the essay.

_____

_____

_____

_____

_____

_____

_____

_____

_____

_____

_____

_____

_____

_____

_____

_____

_____

_____

Look It Over

Review the draft and your revised version of the essay. Think about the corrections or revisions that took the most time. Were they the most important of your revisions or corrections? On a separate sheet of paper, begin a list of the important revisions that take the most time to do. Adding to and studying that list can help you to avoid some problems as you write.

Here's an outline of the key points in Unit 2. Choose the one point in each chapter that you find most helpful to you. Then, jot down words and phrases that tell the meaning of that point.

A. Planning Your Essay

1. How to Think of Ideas   **3.** How to Focus Your Ideas

2. How to Extend an Idea   **4.** How to Organize Information

_____

_____

_____

_____

B. Strategies for Clear and Interesting Writing

1. How to Develop Good Transitions   **3.** How to Structure a Paragraph

2. How to Combine Sentences

_____

_____

_____

_____

C. Mechanics and Usage

1. Sentence Structure, Sentence   **3.** Capitalization and Punctuation
Fragments, and Run-on Sentences

2. Adjectives and Adverbs   **4.** Spelling Hints

_____

_____

_____

_____

D. Revising and Proofreading

Recognize Mistakes, and Decide Which You Have Time to Fix

_____

_____

_____

U N I T 3

PREPARING TO TAKE THE WRITING TEST

What Is a Multiple-Choice Test?

Your writing test may have a section of multiple-choice questions. In this part of the writing test, you will answer numbered questions. After each question you will see four possible answers labeled Ⓐ, Ⓑ, Ⓒ, and Ⓓ. Only one choice is correct. Look at this sample:

Read each sentence. One of the underlined parts is incorrect. Choose the letter that shows where the mistake is.

1. The <u>books</u> that Willy is <u>reading</u> <u>are</u> <u>mine's</u>.
         A   **B** **C** **D**

  Ⓐ A   Ⓒ C
  Ⓑ B   Ⓓ D

The correct answer is Ⓓ. You need to show the answer on the answer sheet.

- Look for **1** on the answer sheet and fill in the space marked Ⓓ.
  Answer Sheet
  1. Ⓐ   Ⓑ   Ⓒ   Ⓓ

Remember these tips:

- Mark all answers on the answer sheet or they won't count.
- Make sure the question number matches the number on the answer sheet.
- Make sure each answer mark is dark and fills its space.
- To change an answer, erase the first mark completely.
- Mark your answers on your answer sheet only.

Strategies for Answering Multiple-Choice Questions

Check It Out

These strategies can help you make the best use of your time. They can also help you make the best choices on a multiple-choice test.

Strategy 1: Read the directions carefully.

Take a deep breath. Make sure you concentrate on the directions. You need to know exactly what you're being asked to do.

Look at this example:

The underlined part of the following sentence may be correct or incorrect. Mark the answer choice that you think is correct.

1. <u>Being that Joan sings the song often</u>, she knows it better than anyone else.
   Ⓐ Being that Joan sings the song often
   Ⓑ Although Joan sings the song often
   Ⓒ Because Joan sings the song often
   Ⓓ However, Joan sings the song often

The directions tell you to decide if the underlined part of the sentence is correct or incorrect. Then choose the correct answer. The underlined part is incorrect. Choice Ⓐ is incorrect because it is the same as the underlined part. Choices Ⓑ and Ⓓ do not make sense and are also incorrect. Reading the directions carefully lets you be certain that the underlined part of the sentence is wrong.

Choice Ⓒ is correct.

Strategy 2: Read all the answer choices for a question before choosing one. Eliminate any answer choices you know are incorrect.

It is important to read all the answer choices before you choose and mark an answer. After you have read all the choices, see if you can eliminate any answers that you know are wrong. Eliminating incorrect answers first gives you a better chance of choosing the correct answer.

Look at this example:

Read the paragraph. Choose the sentence that best states the main idea of the paragraph.

2. Many old ideas about dinosaurs are being challenged today. People once thought dinosaurs were cold-blooded. Dinosaurs also

were thought to be animals that lived by themselves. Some people thought dinosaurs were stupid. New findings suggest that dinosaurs may have been warm-blooded. Dinosaurs may have lived in packs. Other findings suggest that dinosaurs may have been much smarter than people once believed.

Ⓐ Some people thought dinosaurs were stupid.

Ⓑ People once thought dinosaurs were cold-blooded.

Ⓒ Many old ideas about dinosaurs are being challenged today.

Ⓓ Dinosaurs may have lived in packs.

The directions tell you to choose the sentence that best states the main idea of the paragraph. First, look at the choices one by one. Choice Ⓐ is not supported by other sentences. It is incorrect, and you can eliminate it. Choices Ⓑ and Ⓓ are not supported by other sentences. Thus, they are incorrect, and you can eliminate them. Only choice Ⓒ states an idea that is supported by other sentences in the paragraph.

Choice Ⓒ is correct.

Strategy 3: Don't spend too much time on any one question.

You will be graded on the number of right answers you give. For that reason, it's a good idea not to spend too much time on any one question. You might read a question carefully and still be unsure of the answer. In that case, make the best choice you can, and go on to the next question.

Here is one way to figure out how much time to spend on each question. First, find out the total number of multiple-choice questions. Then, divide the number of minutes you have to complete the test by the number of test questions. For example, if you must answer thirty questions during a sixty-minute test, you should spend no more than two minutes on each question.

Work It Out

Now go back over these examples, and mark each answer on the answer sheet your teacher gives you. Make sure your answers are dark and completely fill their spaces.

Look It Over

Which strategy do you think will be most useful in taking multiple-choice tests? On a separate sheet of paper, write the strategy, and explain why you think it will be useful.

Practice a Multiple-Choice Test

Remember that practice in answering multiple-choice questions will improve your test-taking skills.

Check It Out

In this lesson, you will practice answering different kinds of multiple-choice questions. Your teacher will give you an answer sheet. Be careful as you mark it.

Work It Out

Allow yourself fifteen minutes to answer all the questions that follow.

Choose the best supporting detail for the underlined main idea.

1. A storm seems to be approaching.
   - Ⓐ I had frankfurters for lunch.
   - Ⓑ The sky is darkening, and the wind is rising.
   - Ⓒ We had a storm on the same day last year.
   - Ⓓ Rain fell yesterday.

Read the numbered sentences. Choose the answer that shows the most logical order of the sentences for a paragraph.

2. 1. I added the roof as the final touch.
   2. I studied the plans for the birdhouse.
   3. I built the bottom floor.
   4. I attached the walls, one with an entrance.
   - Ⓐ 4-3-2-1
   - Ⓑ 3-2-1-4
   - Ⓒ 3-4-1-2
   - Ⓓ 2-3-4-1

Read the paragraph. Choose the answer that shows the mistake.

3. I joined my friends on a hiking trip. My younger sister came along, to. Our first day out, we had a thunderstorm. That night, one of the tents collapsed.
   - Ⓐ hiking
   - Ⓑ to
   - Ⓒ thunderstorm
   - Ⓓ tents

Read the paragraph. Choose the letter of the sentence that does not belong in the paragraph.

4. My brother and I tried to set up a theater in our yard. **(A)** We built a stage, hung a curtain, and set up chairs. **(B)** I practiced hockey for an hour. **(C)** We set up a ticket booth. **(D)** Before we sold a single ticket, the stage collapsed.

   Ⓐ A
   Ⓑ B
   Ⓒ C
   Ⓓ D

The underlined part of the sentence may be correct or incorrect. Choose the answer you think is correct.

5. The two dogs and three neighborhood cats has been fighting in the backyard.

   Ⓐ has fought
   Ⓑ fights
   Ⓒ have been fighting
   Ⓓ has been fighting

Read the sentences. Choose the best transition from the first sentence to the second.

6. Sara had almost completed her ice-skating program. _____, the blade on her left skate came loose only moments before her final jump and spin.

   Ⓐ In addition
   Ⓑ Unfortunately
   Ⓒ Fortunately
   Ⓓ On the other hand

Look It Over

Which kinds of multiple-choice directions and questions did you find the most difficult? Review the strategies for answering multiple-choice questions. On a separate sheet of paper, write a few sentences about how you might better apply the strategies when you take multiple-choice tests.

Now you're ready to practice taking both parts of a writing test. You will write an essay and then take a multiple-choice test. Remember to pay careful attention to the essay prompt and to the directions for the multiple-choice questions.

General Directions

In this part of the writing test, you will write an essay based on the prompt. You will have thirty minutes to complete your essay. Read the prompt, then spend a few minutes thinking about the prompt and organizing your thoughts. Make your plans or notes on a separate sheet of paper. Then, on a clean sheet of paper, write your essay. Use a #2 pencil or a pen. Allow a few minutes at the end for revising and proofreading.

Essay Topic

> *Choose a place where you enjoy spending time. Write an essay that describes the place. Include as many kinds of details as you can to help the reader form a mental picture of the place.*

Multiple-Choice Portion

In this part of the writing test, you'll answer multiple-choice questions. Read the directions for each question carefully. Mark all of your answers on the answer sheet. Mark only one answer for each question. If you change an answer, erase the first answer completely. If you do not know the answer to a question, make the best choice you can. Then move on to the next question. You have twenty-five minutes.

Read the following paragraph. Choose the letter of the sentence that does not belong in the paragraph.

1. **(A)** We watched the sunset from the big window at the back of the restaurant. **(B)** The huge, red circle seemed to sink slowly into the lake. **(C)** The restaurant was not far from the highway. **(D)** As the sun began to disappear, the sky became orange.

   Ⓐ A
   Ⓑ B
   Ⓒ C
   Ⓓ D

Read the paragraph. Choose the sentence that best states its main idea.

2. Public schools offer everyone a chance to get an education. Police and fire departments help protect us against injuries. Public libraries provide books for us to borrow and read.
   - Ⓐ Governments should lower taxes whenever possible.
   - Ⓑ Government services help protect and improve our lives.
   - Ⓒ Public schools enrich a community.
   - Ⓓ People deserve police protection.

The sentence below is the main idea of a paragraph. Choose the sentence that would work best as a supporting detail.

3. People have different reasons for dressing the way they do.
   - Ⓐ Good clothes do not fit most young people.
   - Ⓑ I buy most of my clothes at discount stores.
   - Ⓒ Clothes can be a way of expressing your personality.
   - Ⓓ The history of clothing is interesting.

Directions for questions 4-5:

Choose the best way to combine the ideas into one sentence.

4. The chef put eggs into the bowl. She put salt into the bowl. She put pepper into the bowl. She mixed all these ingredients.
   - Ⓐ The chef put eggs, salt, and pepper into the bowl.
   - Ⓑ The chef put eggs, salt, and pepper into the bowl and mixed them all.
   - Ⓒ The chef put eggs, salt, and pepper into the bowl, she mixed them all.
   - Ⓓ The chef put eggs into the bowl and salt and pepper into the bowl and mixed them all.

5. Sandy saw the rain. She left without a raincoat.
   - Ⓐ Sandy saw the rain, she left without a raincoat.
   - Ⓑ Sandy saw the rain, if she left without a raincoat.
   - Ⓒ However Sandy saw the rain, she left without a raincoat.
   - Ⓓ Although Sandy saw the rain, she left without a raincoat.

Directions for questions 6-7:

Each sentence below has an underlined part that may be correct or incorrect. Choose the answer you think is correct.

6. If he dances <u>good</u> enough, he will get into the show.
   - Ⓐ good
   - Ⓑ better
   - Ⓒ best
   - Ⓓ well

7. No one <u>believes</u> the story he told us last night.
   - Ⓐ believes
   - Ⓑ beleives
   - Ⓒ bielieves
   - Ⓓ believe

Directions for questions 8-9:

Each sentence has one underlined word that needs to be corrected. Mark the letter that shows where the error is located.

8. Sylvia <u>didnt</u> want to <u>collect</u> the <u>signatures</u> for <u>Alan's</u> petition.
   - Ⓐ didnt
   - Ⓑ collect
   - Ⓒ signatures
   - Ⓓ Alan's

9. He <u>prefers</u> rock, <u>where</u> I <u>like</u> country <u>music</u>.
   - Ⓐ prefers
   - Ⓑ where
   - Ⓒ like
   - Ⓓ music

Directions for questions 10-11:

Read each sentence below. Choose the letter that shows the mistake.

10.   A   B   C   D
    "<u>It's</u> never going to be <u>finished</u>," Jaclyn <u>said</u>, <u>slaming</u> the door behind her.
   - Ⓐ A
   - Ⓑ B
   - Ⓒ C
   - Ⓓ D

11.   A   B   C   D
    One of the <u>teachers</u> <u>were</u> going to <u>sell</u> tickets <u>at</u> the door.
   - Ⓐ A
   - Ⓑ B
   - Ⓒ C
   - Ⓓ D

Look It Over

As you look over the practice writing test you just finished, think about the questions below. Answering them will give you an idea of what kinds of things you need to practice.

The Essay

When you have finished your essay, read it carefully. Then use the scoring scale to see how well you did.

Circle a number on the scale after each question. (**5** is the highest you can score; **1** is the lowest.)

Does the essay answer the prompt clearly and completely?

1　2　3　4　5

Do the main ideas in the essay relate to the central idea?

1　2　3　4　5

Do the details in the essay support the main ideas?

1　2　3　4　5

Is the essay organized in paragraphs that are clear and easy to follow?

1　2　3　4　5

Do the ideas flow smoothly from one to another?

1　2　3　4　5

Is the essay free of errors in sentence structure, capitalization, and punctuation?

1　2　3　4　5

Now find out how you did on the multiple-choice part of the test.

The Multiple-Choice Questions

With your teacher, review your scored test. Pay close attention to any mistakes you made. On a separate sheet of paper, list the questions on which you made mistakes. Then list ideas about how you can improve your skills in answering multiple-choice questions. Review the strategies for answering multiple-choice questions.

Think It Over

What do you think is the most important strategy you will take into the test with you? Why is this strategy so important for you? Write your ideas on a separate sheet of paper.

Here is an outline of the key points in Unit 3. After you look over the whole outline, jot down your thoughts about why it is important to use each strategy. These notes are for your own use, so don't worry about writing complete sentences.

Strategies for Answering Multiple-Choice Questions

1. Read the directions carefully.

_____

_____

_____

_____

_____

_____

2. Read all the answer choices before choosing one. Identify wrong answers first. Then choose the right answer.

_____

_____

_____

_____

_____

_____

3. Don't get stuck on one question. Make the best choice you can, then move on to the next question.

_____

_____

_____

_____

_____

A business letter has six parts.

1. **Heading:** your address and the date

2. **Inside address:** name and title of the individual you are writing; address of the company where that person works

3. **Salutation:** greeting and name of the person that you are writing

4. **Body:** your message

5. **Closing:** the closing greeting

6. **Signature:** your name

Here is an example of a business letter:

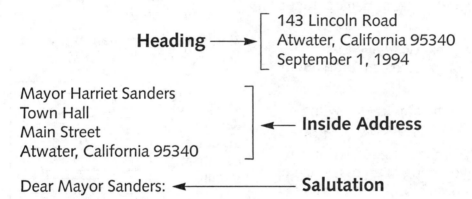

Heading →
```
143 Lincoln Road
Atwater, California 95340
September 1, 1994
```

Mayor Harriet Sanders
Town Hall
Main Street
Atwater, California 95340

← **Inside Address**

Dear Mayor Sanders: ← **Salutation**

I wonder if you can help get a street light put in on Lincoln Road.

In the past two years, eight houses were built on Lincoln Road. Many children live and play in this neighborhood. Yet there aren't any street lights south of Berry Street. Cars traveling along Lincoln Road are a danger to these children. If a street light is put in, the street will be safer for everyone.

Can you please look into this problem and think about my suggestion?

← **Body**

Closing → Sincerely,

Signature → *Melissa Evans*

Melissa Evans

Adjective: words used to describe nouns or pronouns

Adverb: words used to describe verbs, adjectives, or other adverbs

Body: middle part of an essay

Central idea: most important idea of an essay

Closing: last paragraph of an essay

Descriptive essay: essay that describes a person, place, or thing

Detail web: way to organize details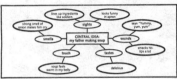

Essay: short piece of writing about a topic

Expository essay: essay that explains or gives information about a topic

Extend: to fill out an idea with information and details

Focus: element of good writing in which everything in an essay relates to the central idea

Introduction: first paragraph of an essay; this paragraph states the central idea

Multiple-choice test: test that gives three or more answer choices

Narrative essay: an essay that tells a story

Organization: ordering an essay to start with the central idea, include supporting details and conclude with the central idea

Persuasive essay: essay that gives an opinion about an idea and tries to make the reader agree with that opinion

Plural subject: names more than one person, place, thing, or idea

Process: a series of steps that leads to a finished product

Prompt: statement on a writing test that gives the writing topic

Revise: change an essay to improve it

Run-on sentence: two or more sentences joined incorrectly

Sentence: group of words that expresses a complete thought and contains a subject and a verb

Sentence fragment: group of words that does not express a complete thought

Singular subject: names one person, place, thing, or idea

Story map: way to organize events and details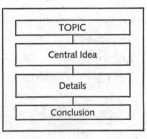

Subject: the person, place, thing, or idea that a sentence is about

Support: main ideas and details that back up the central idea of an essay

Topic sentence: sentence that expresses the main idea of an essay

Transition: word or phrase that connects two ideas or sentences

Verb: word that tells what the subject of a sentence does or is